My Vehicle Coloring Book

This book includes two copies of each illustration, for even more colouring fun!

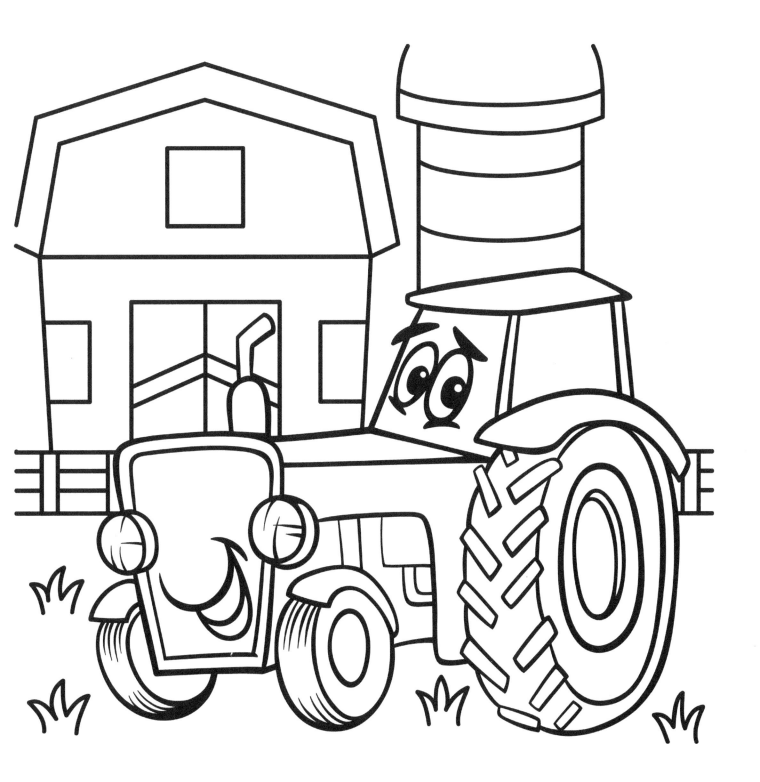

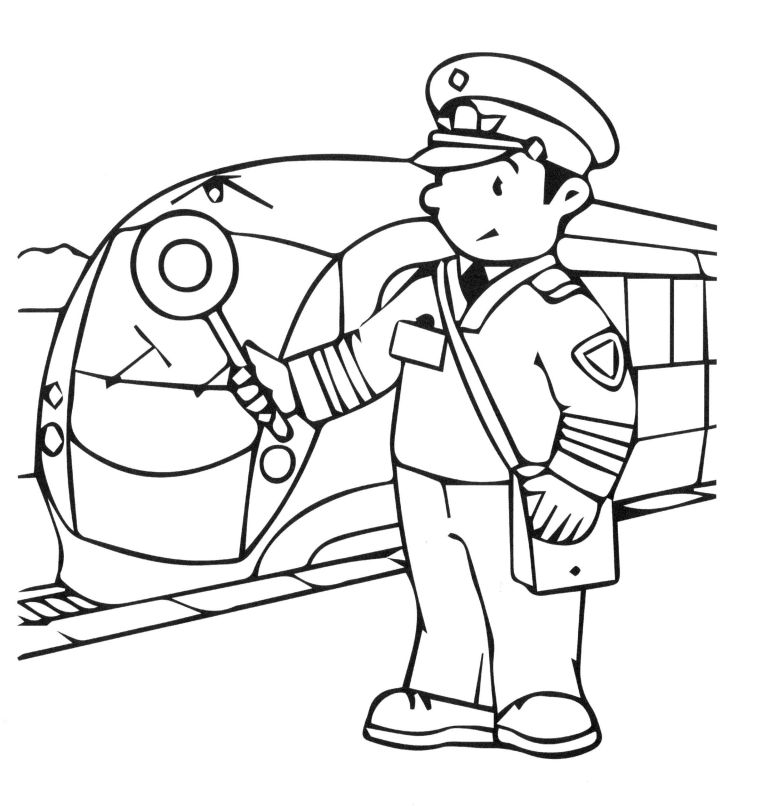

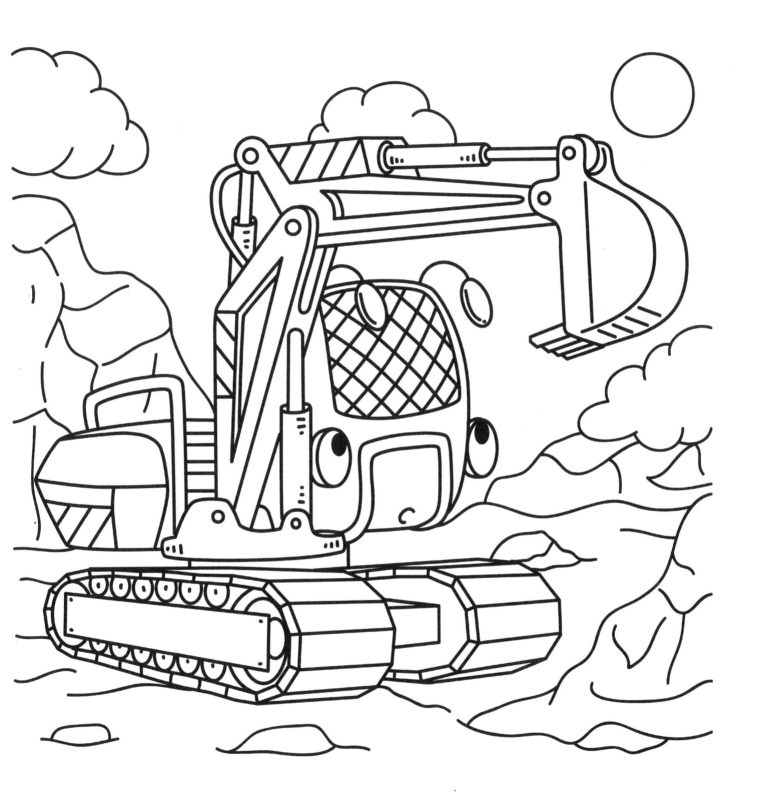

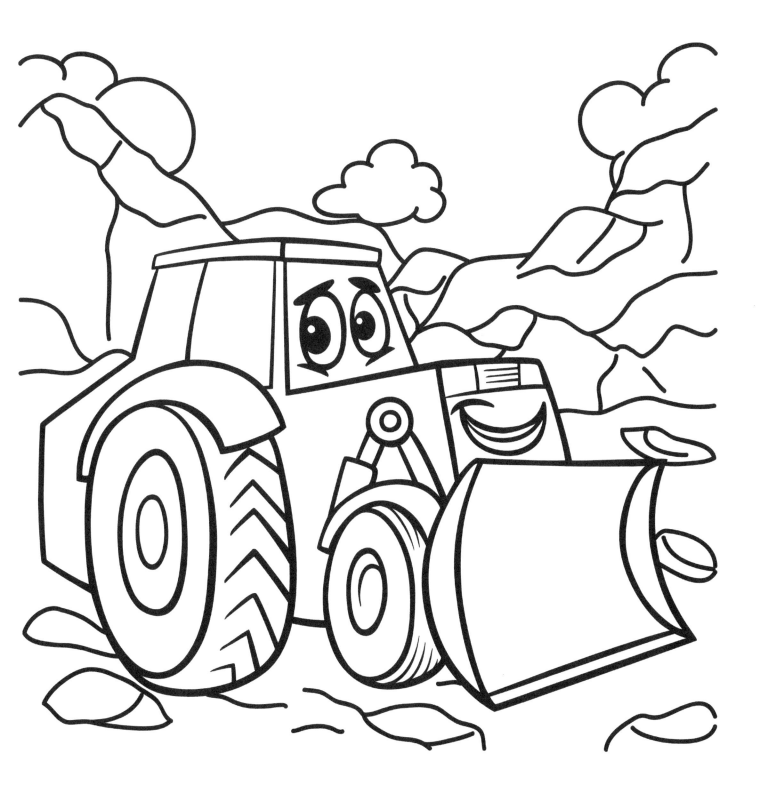

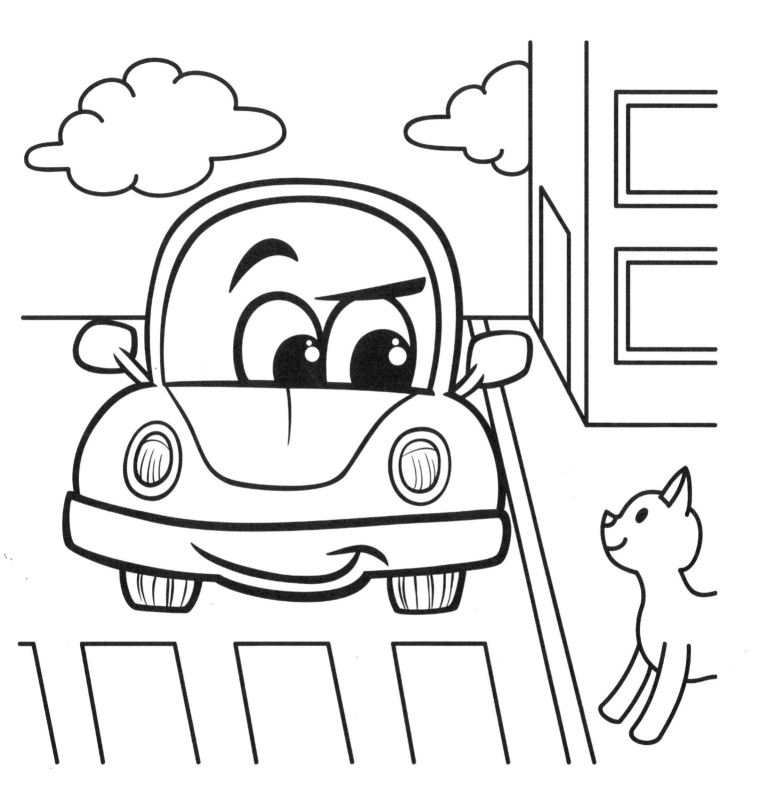

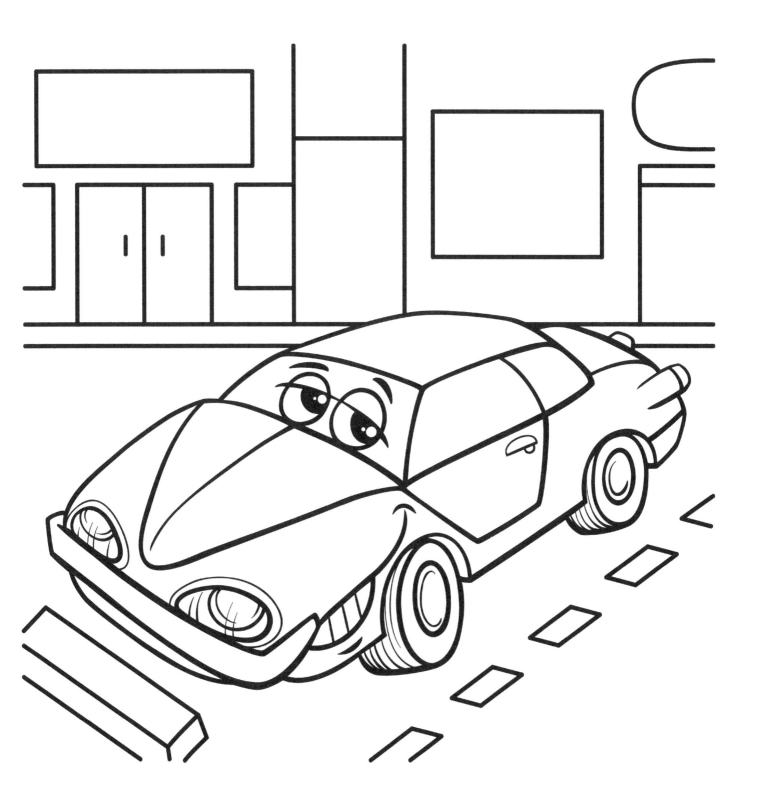

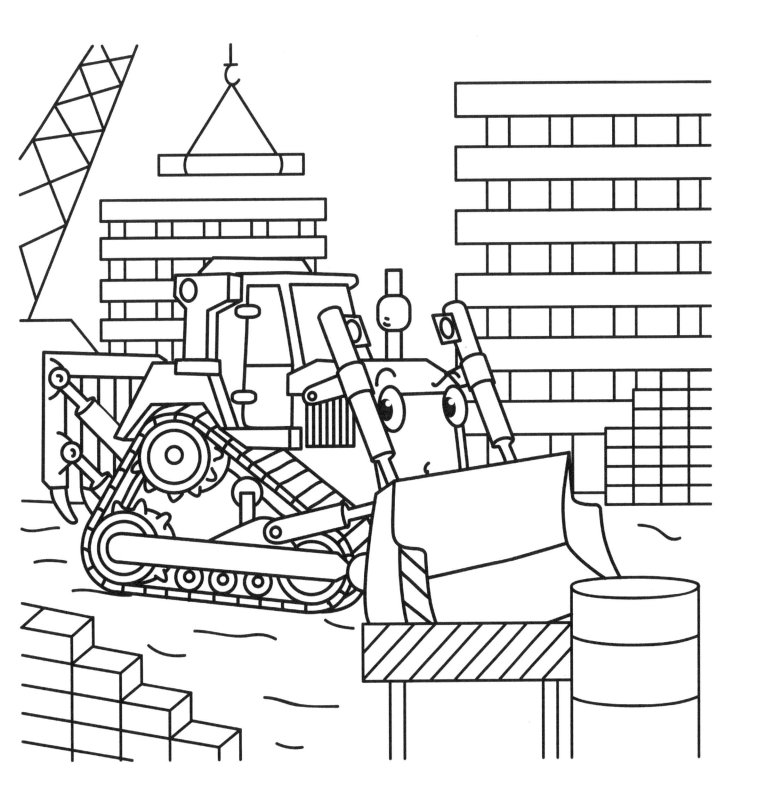

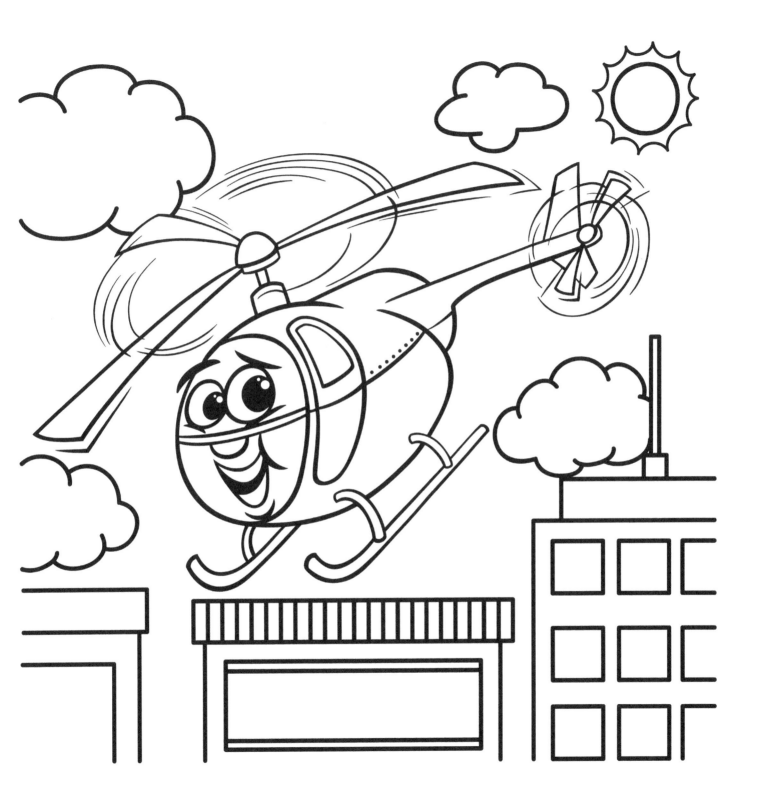

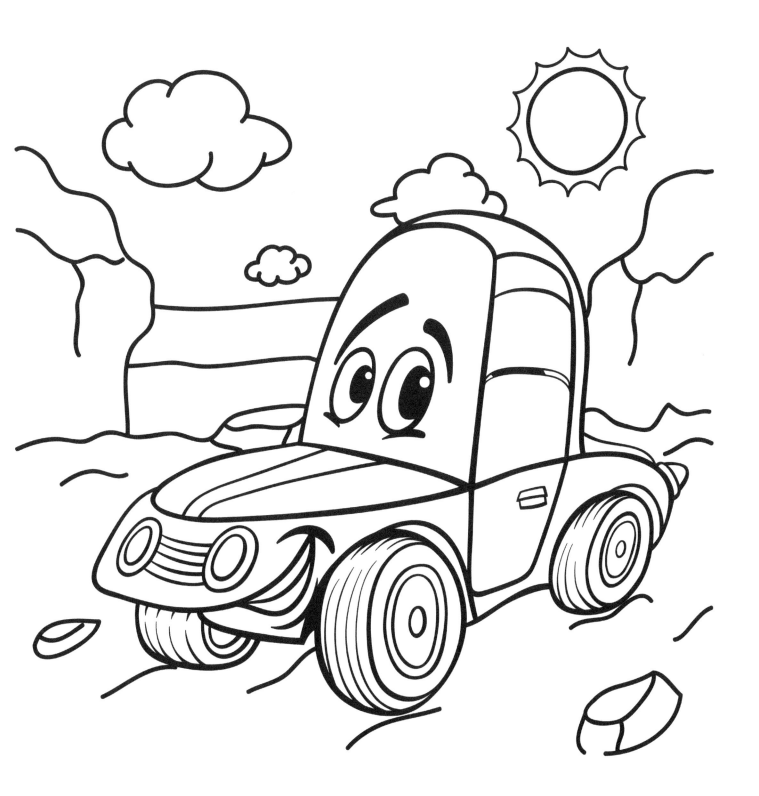

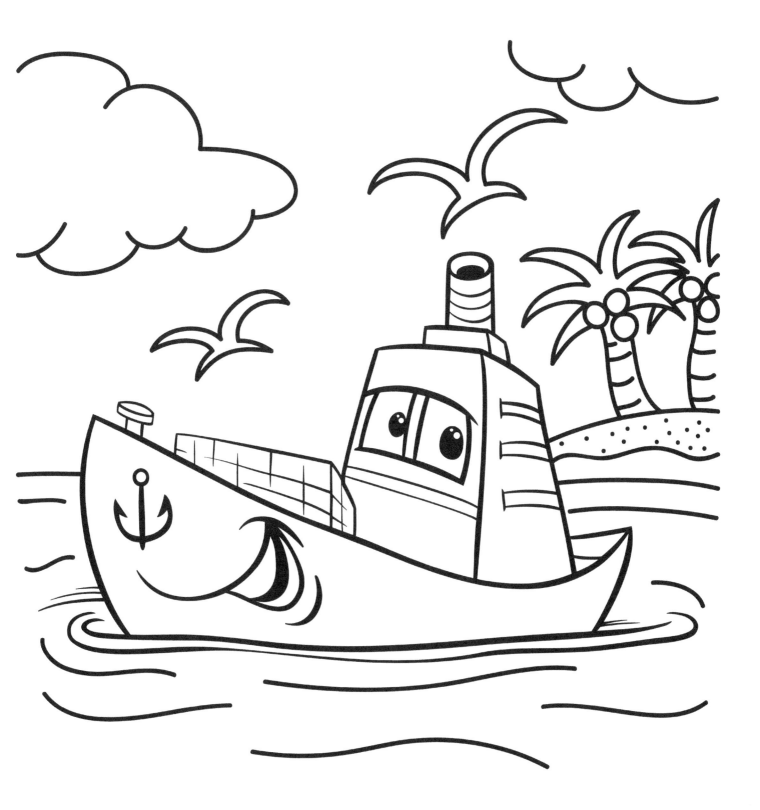

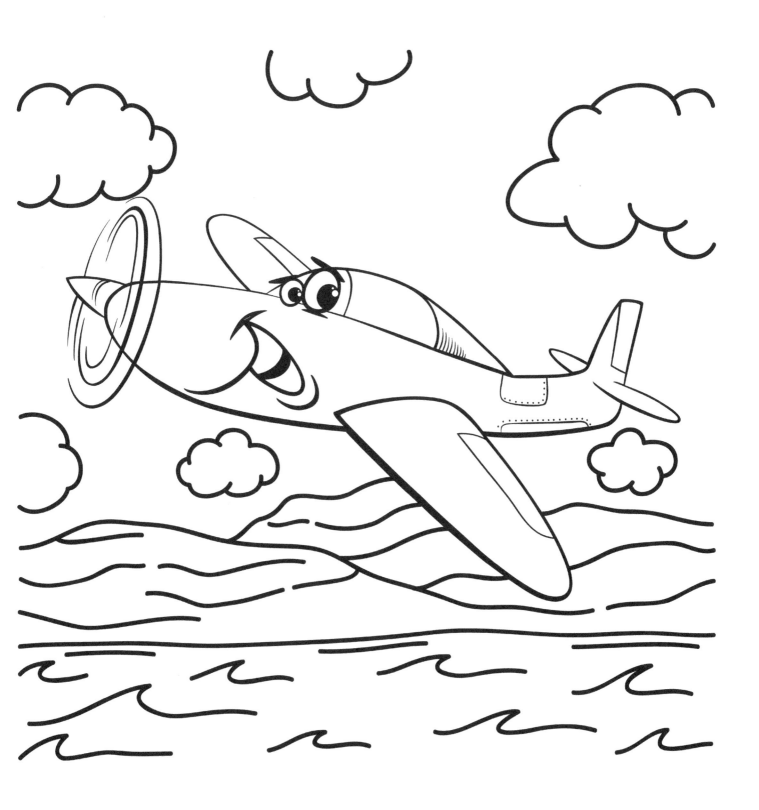

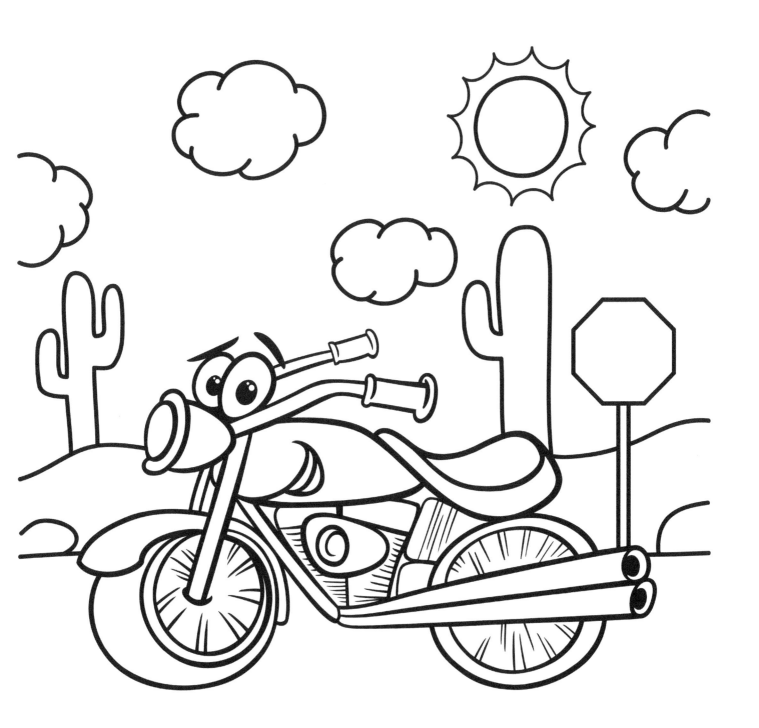

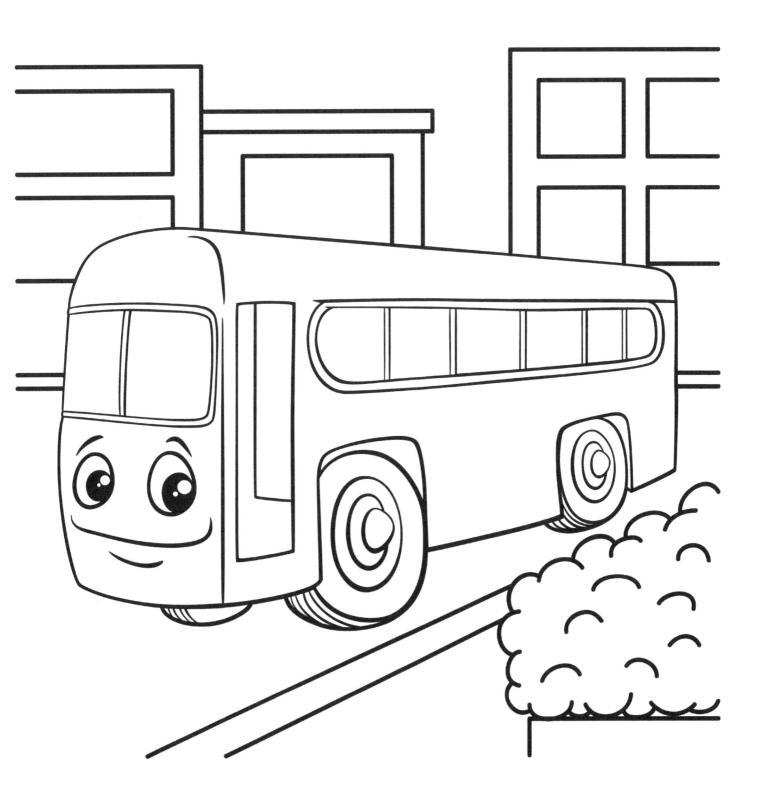

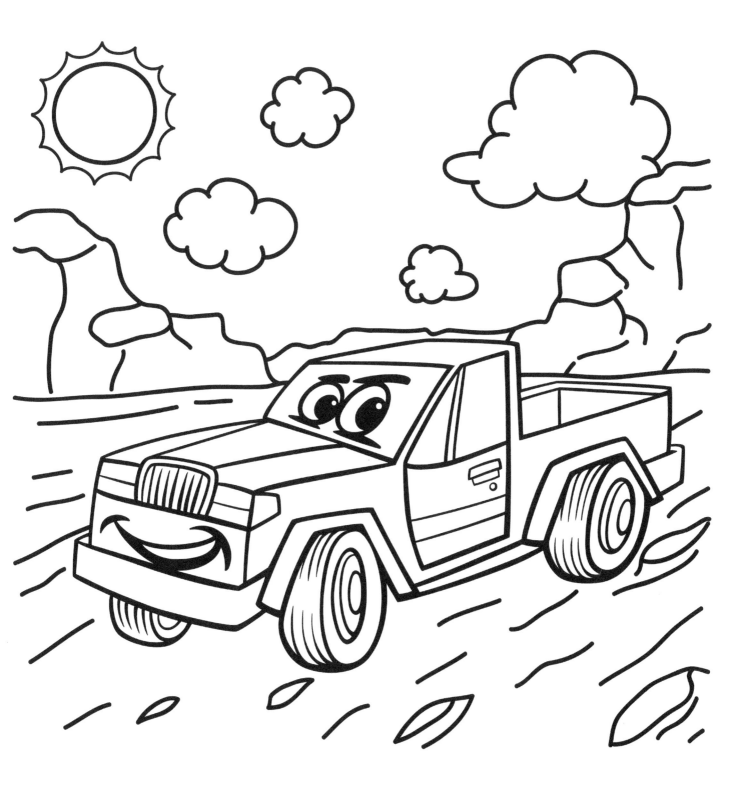

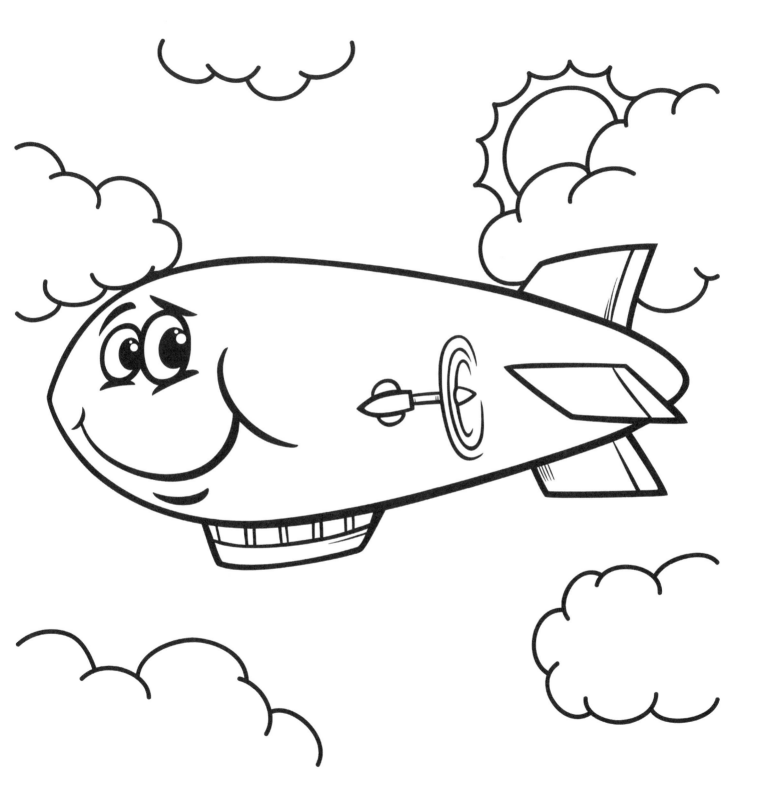

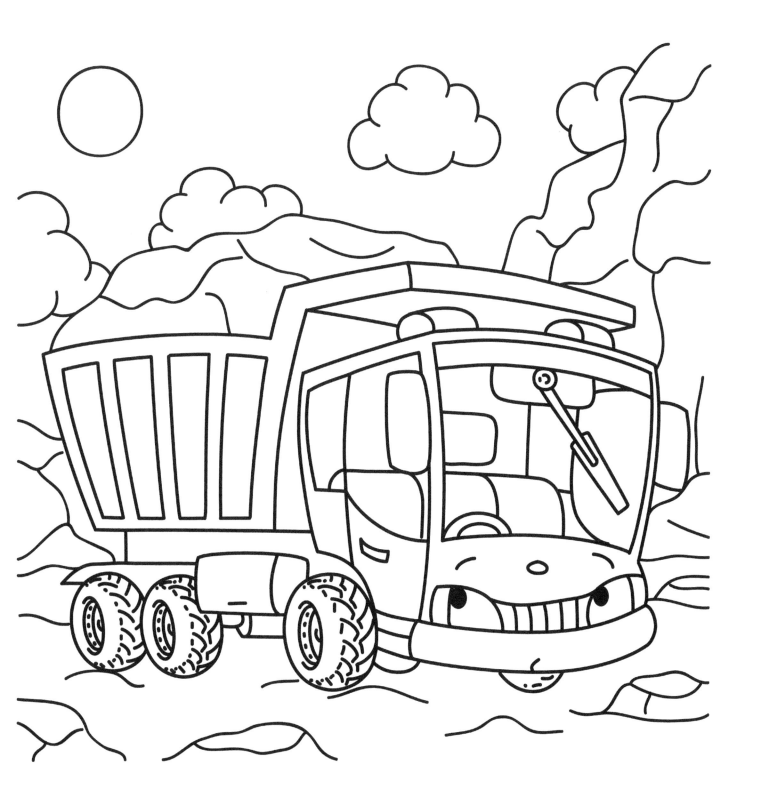

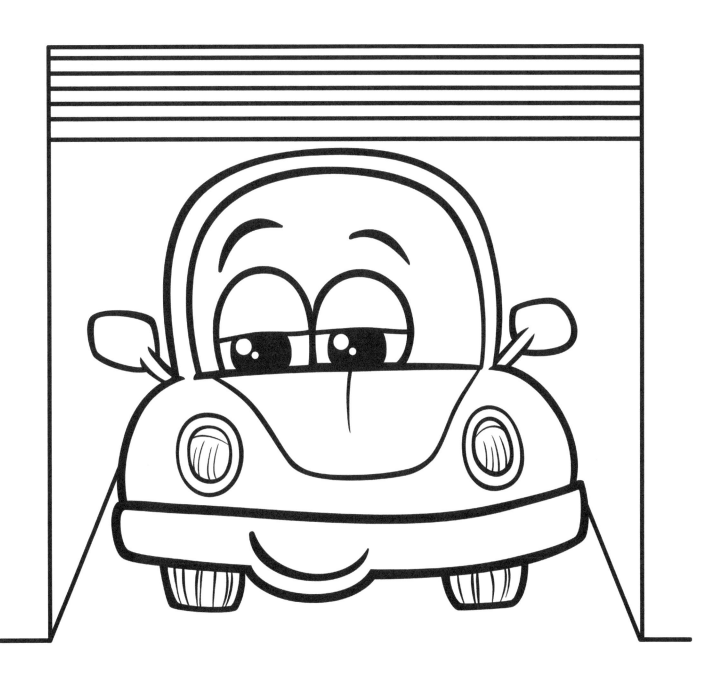

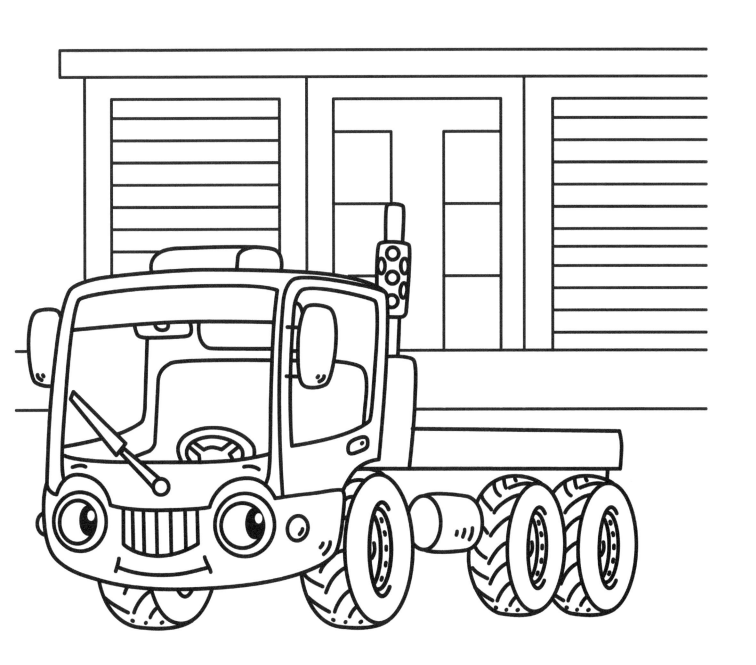

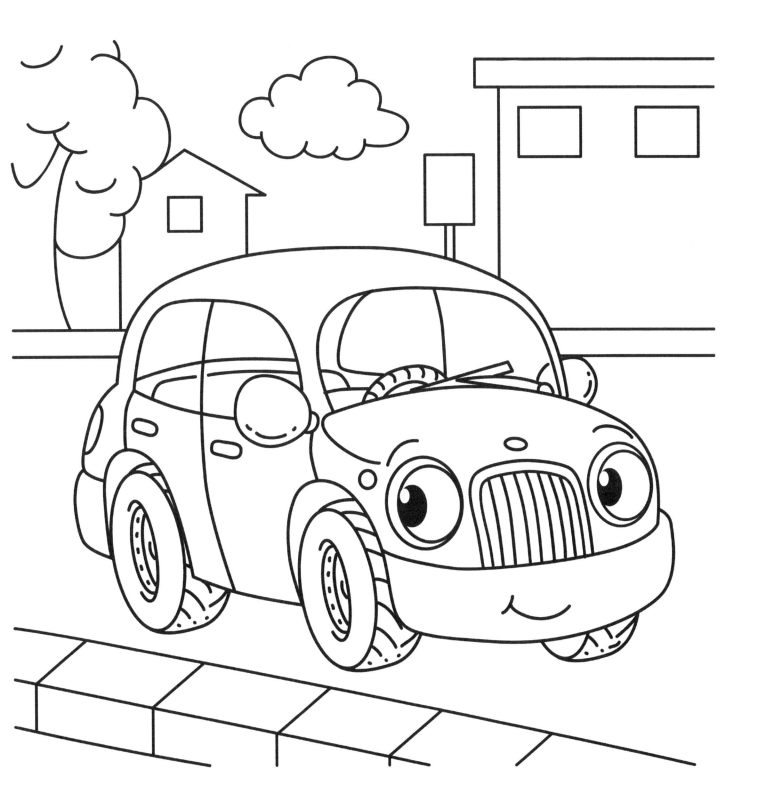

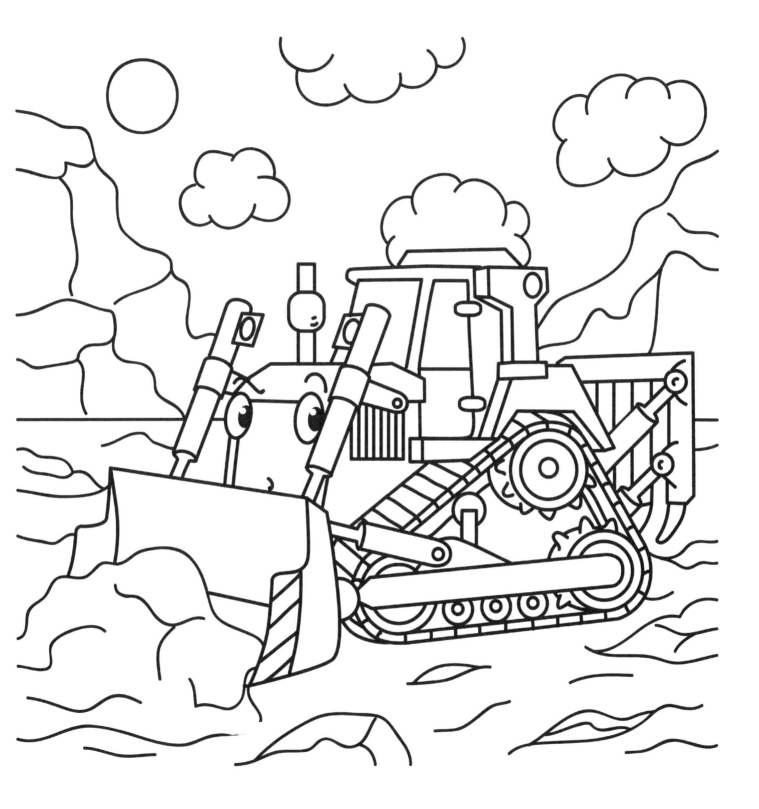

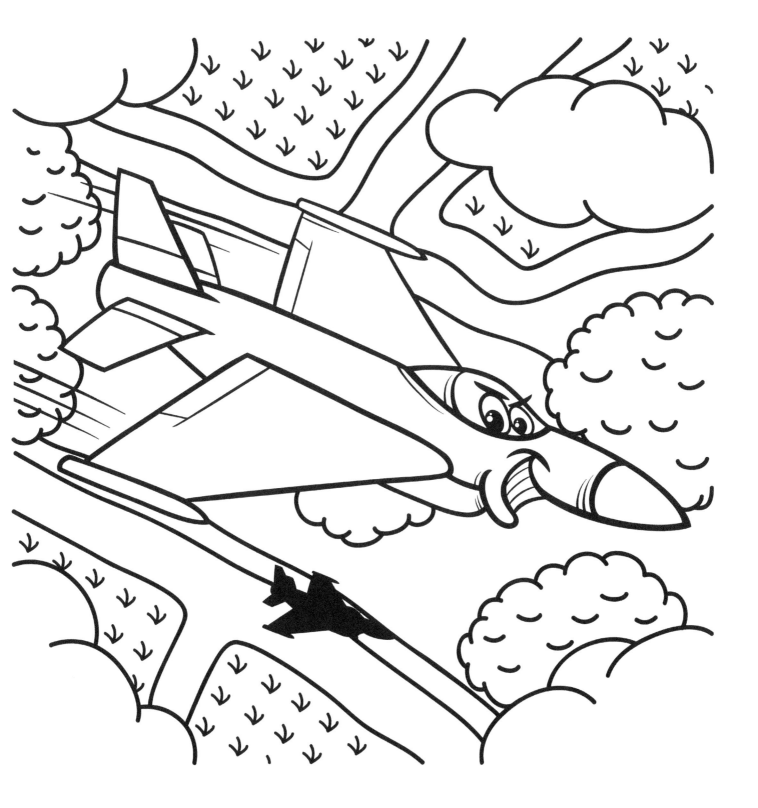

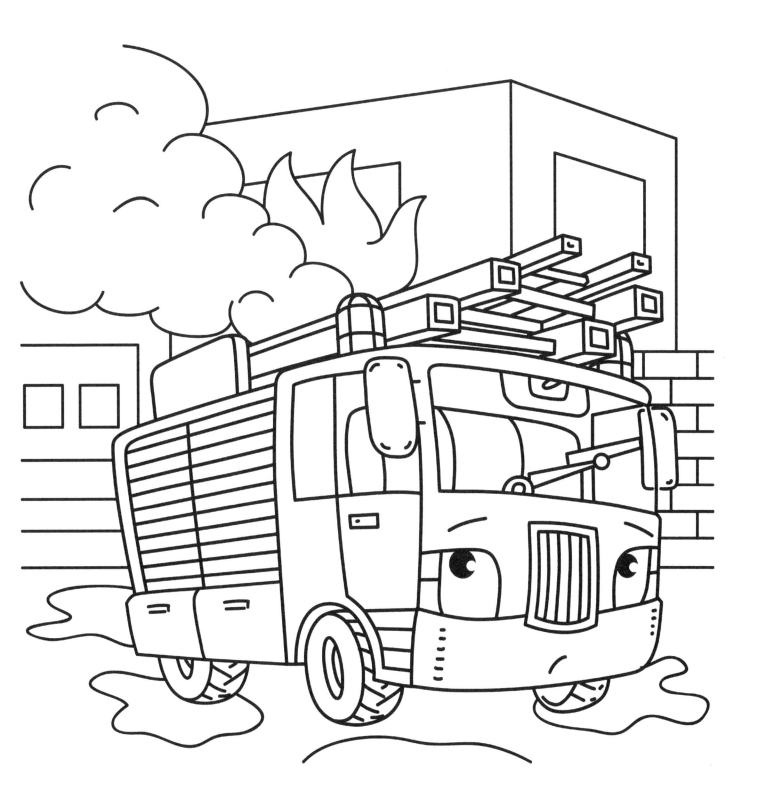

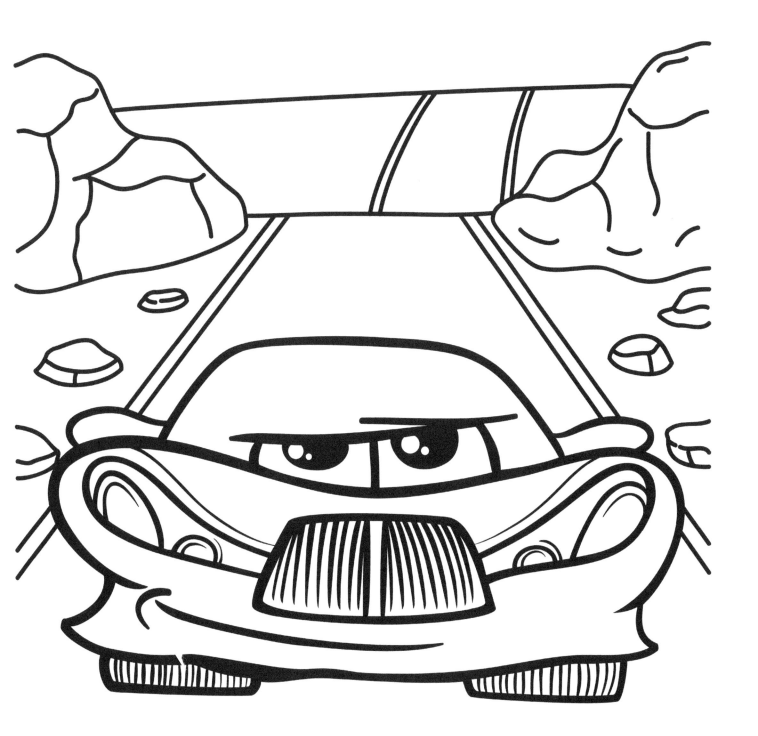

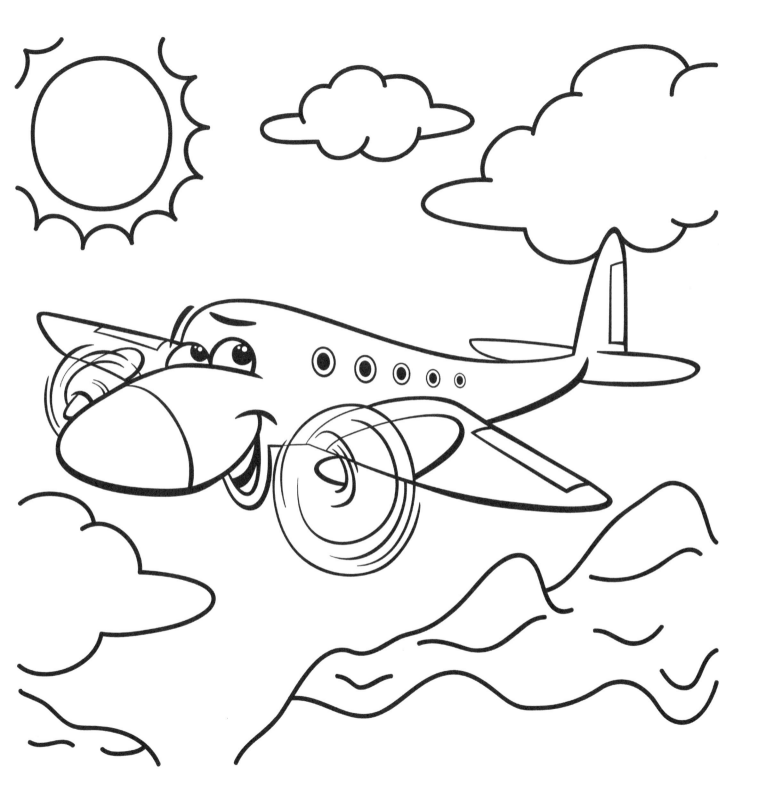

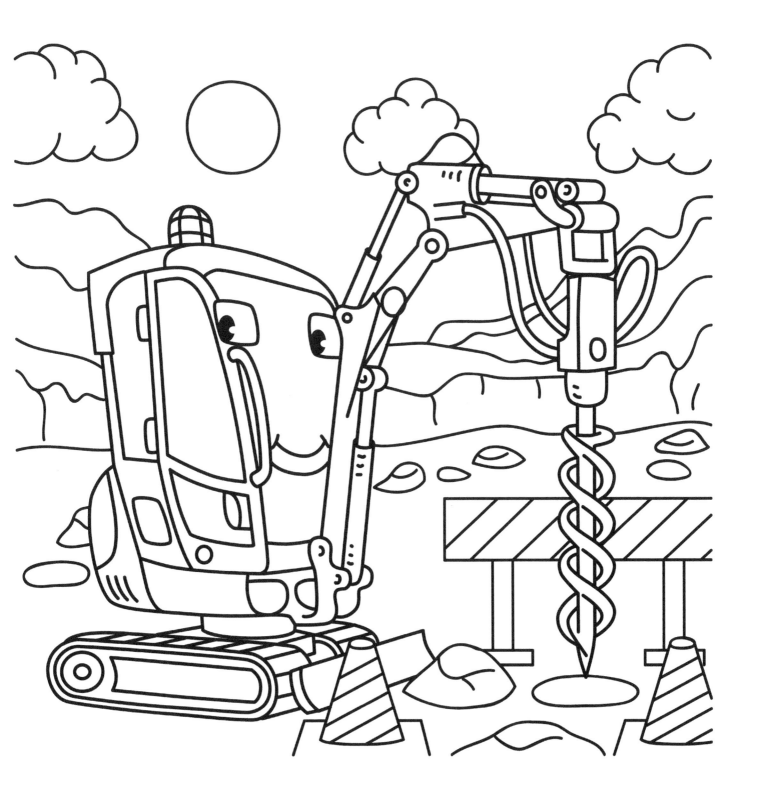

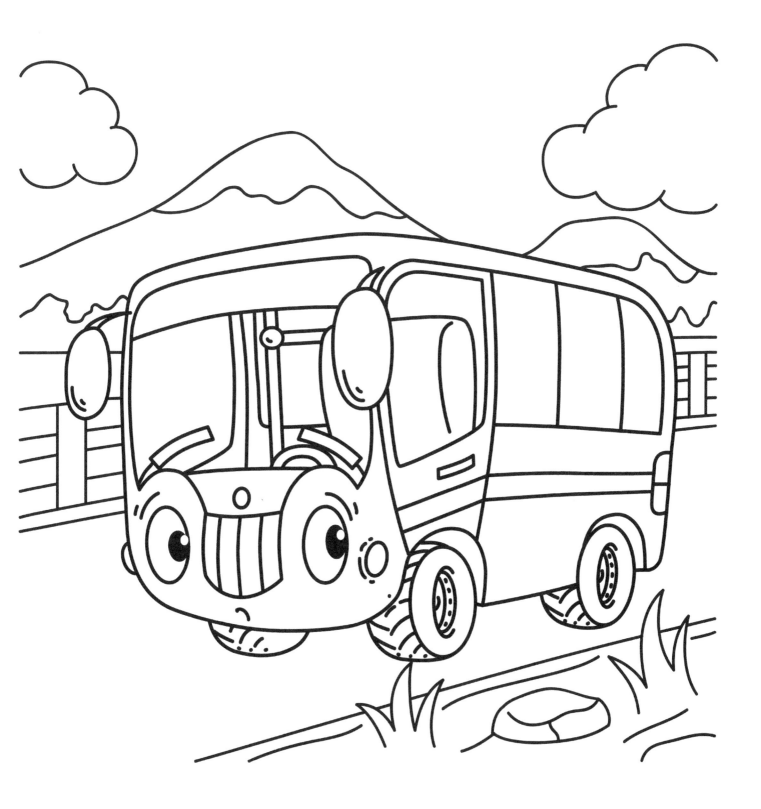

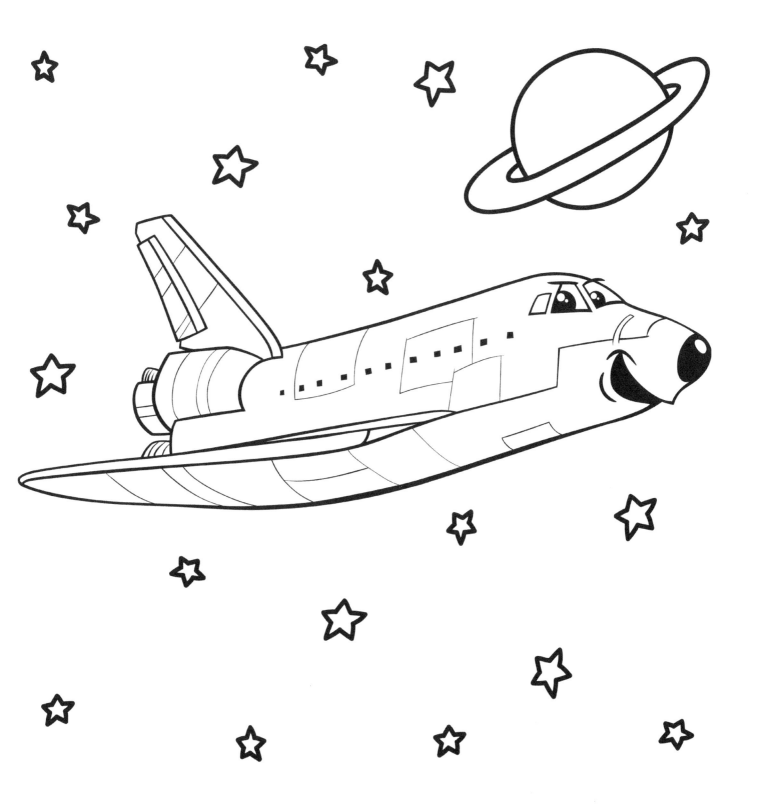

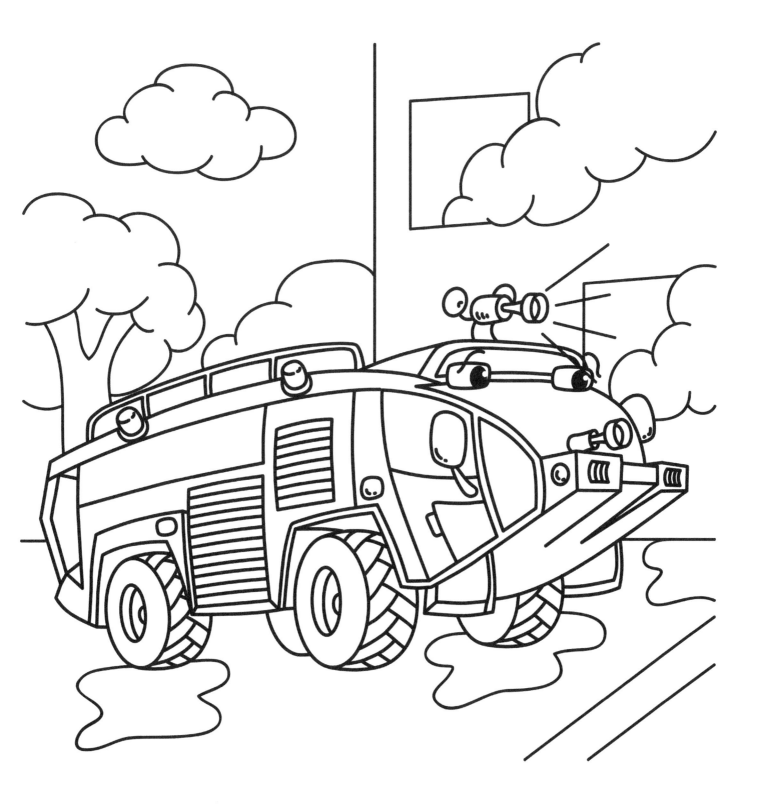

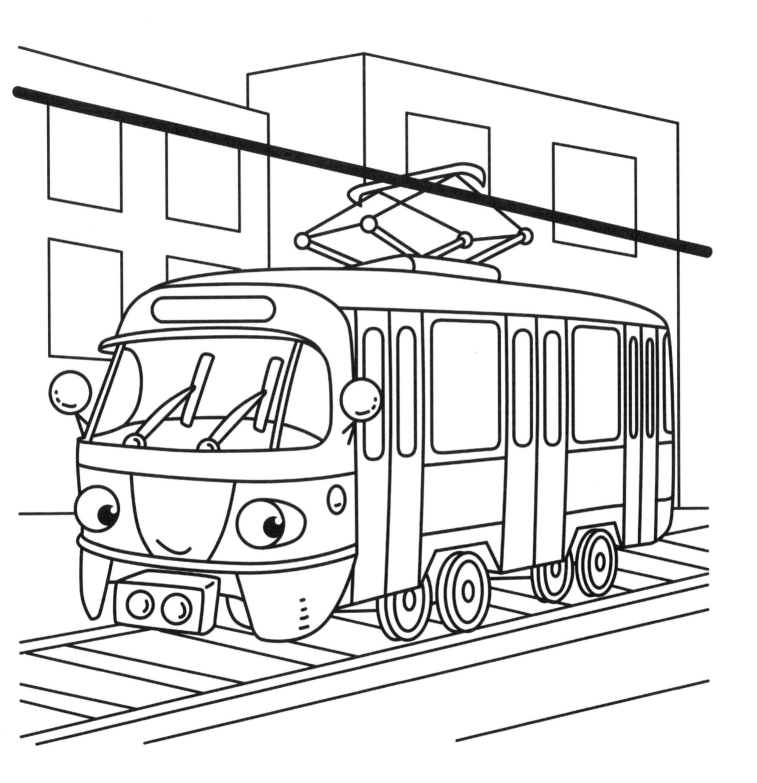

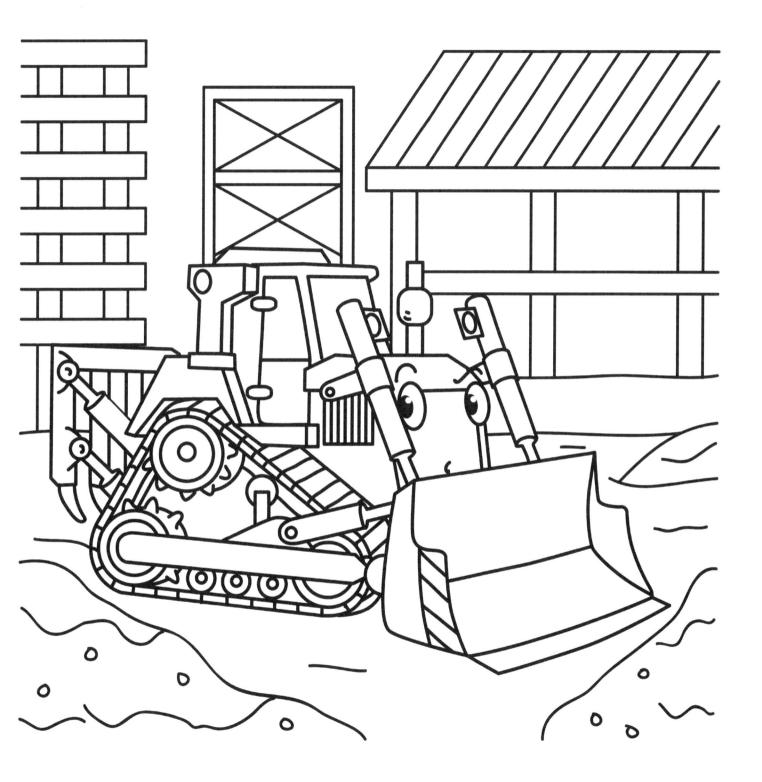

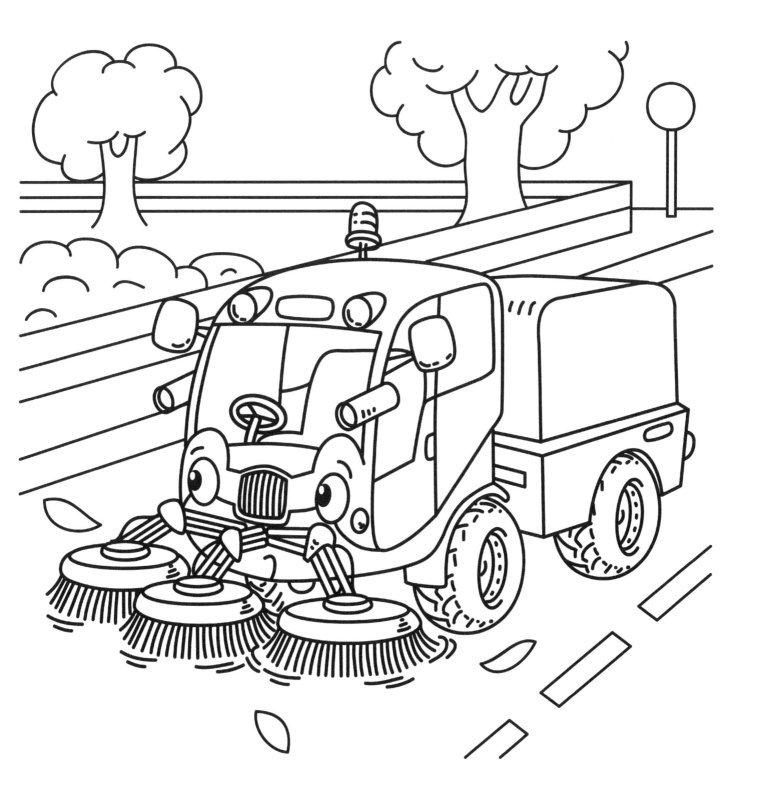

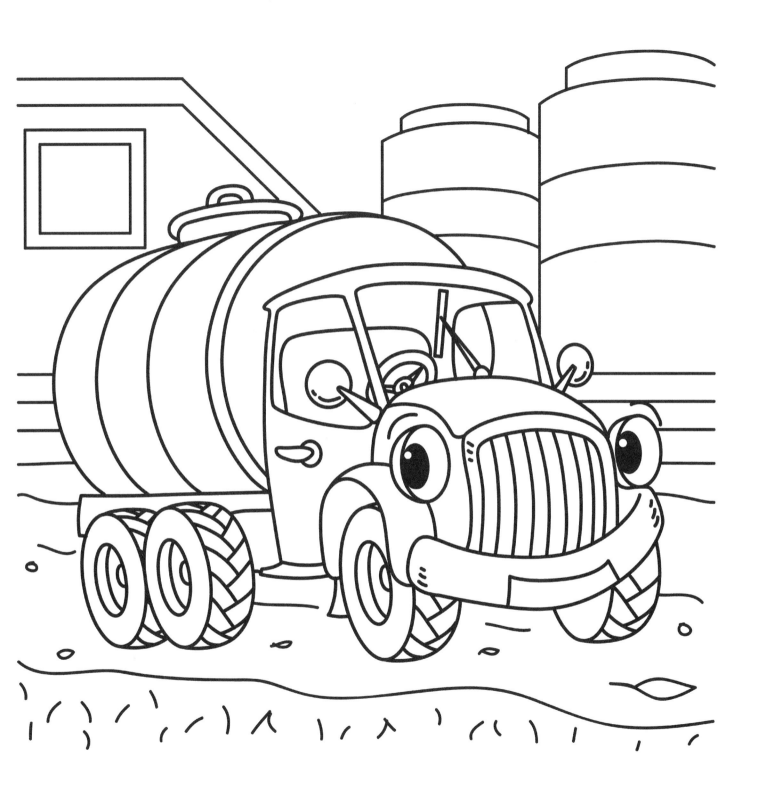

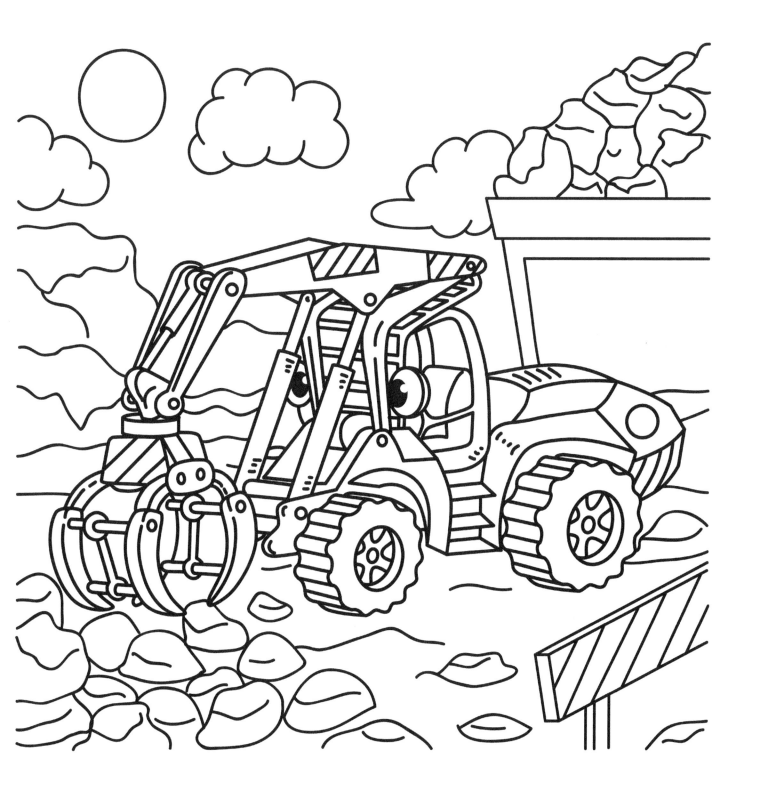

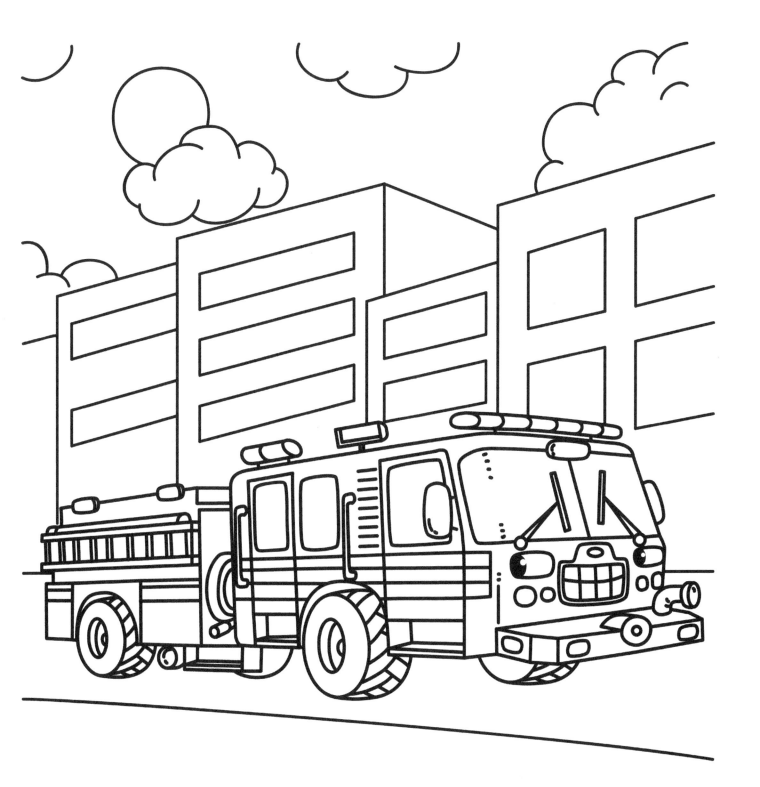

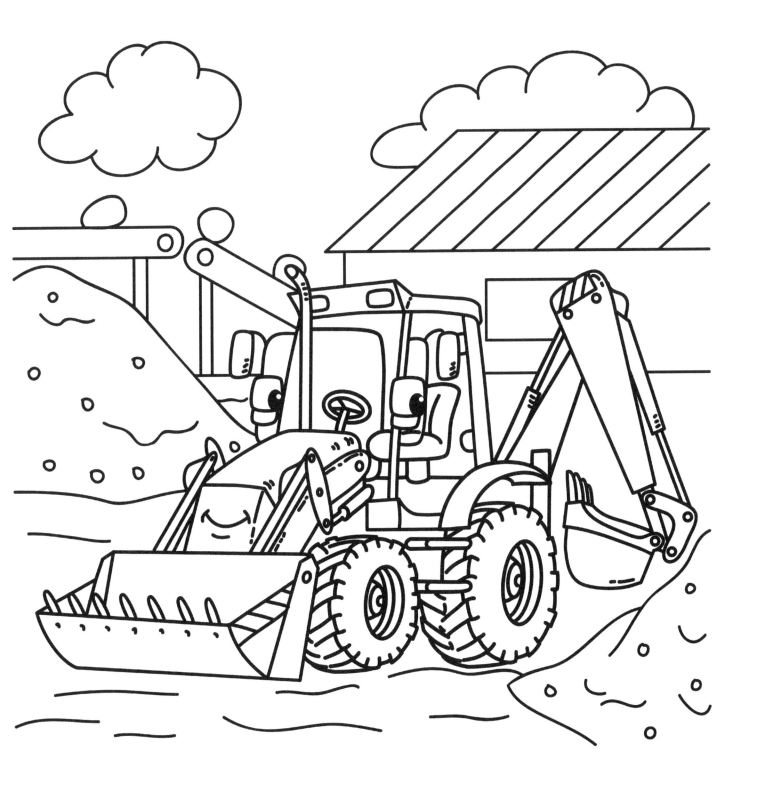

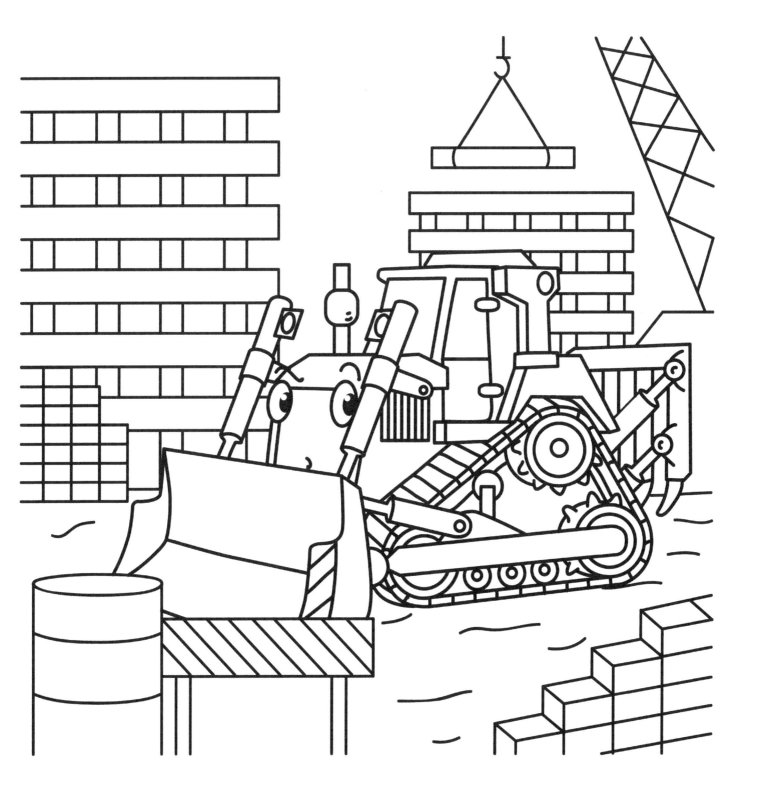

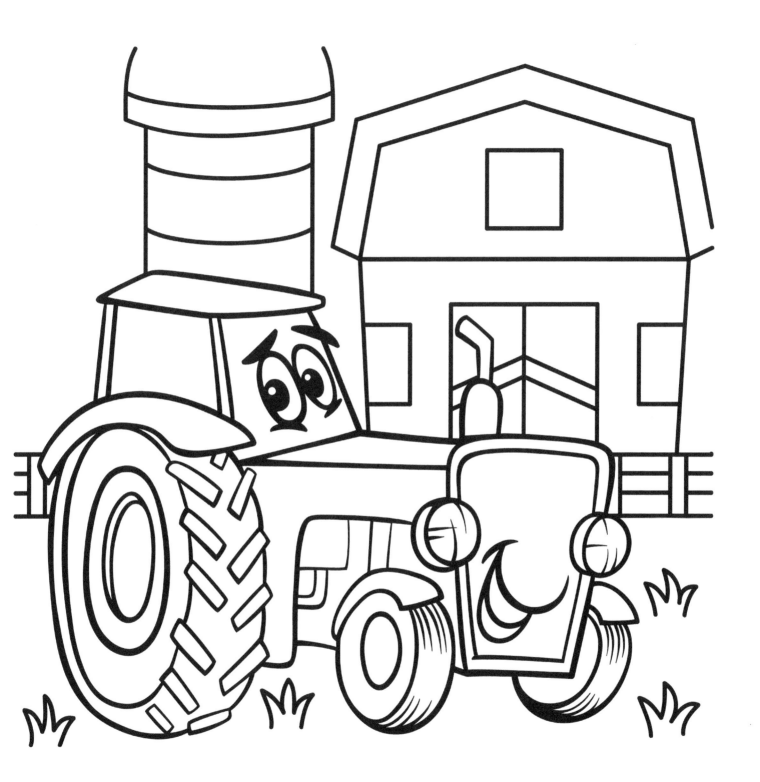

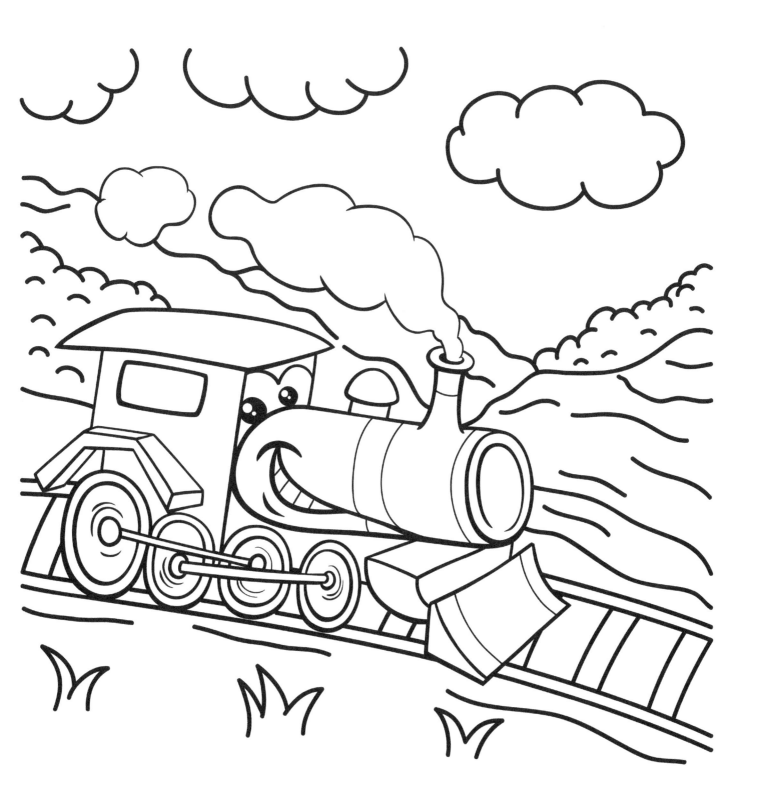

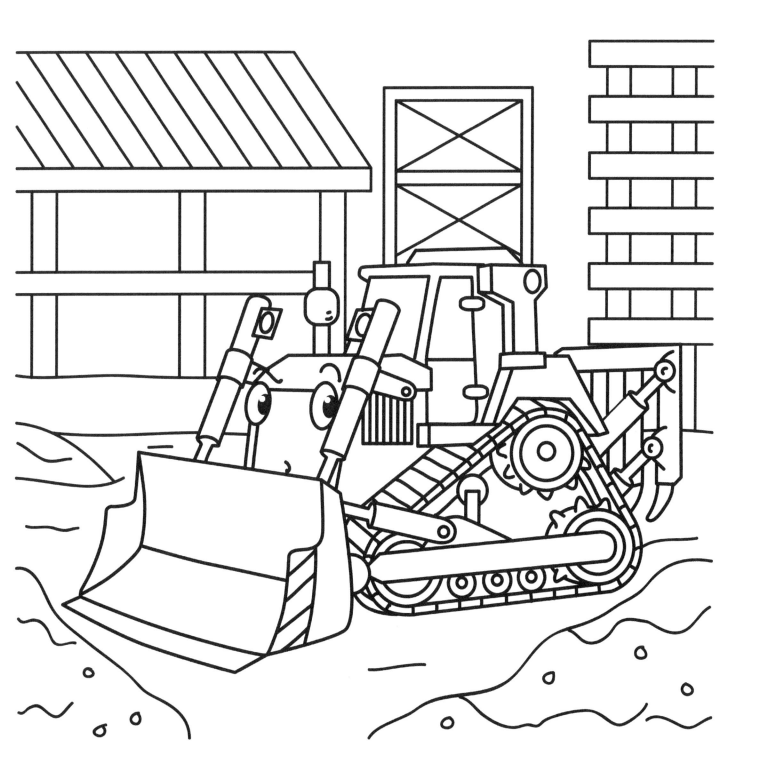

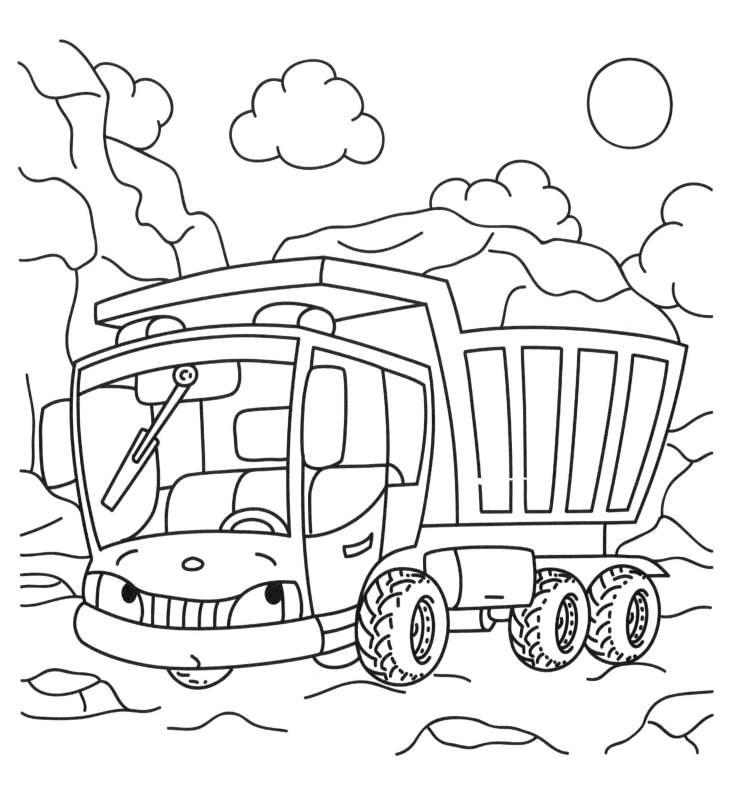

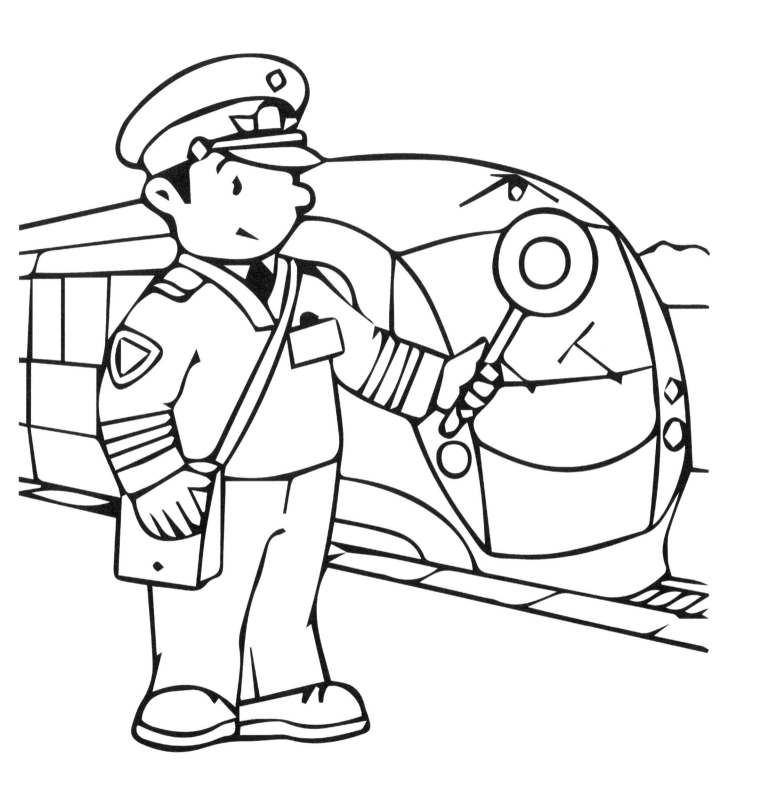

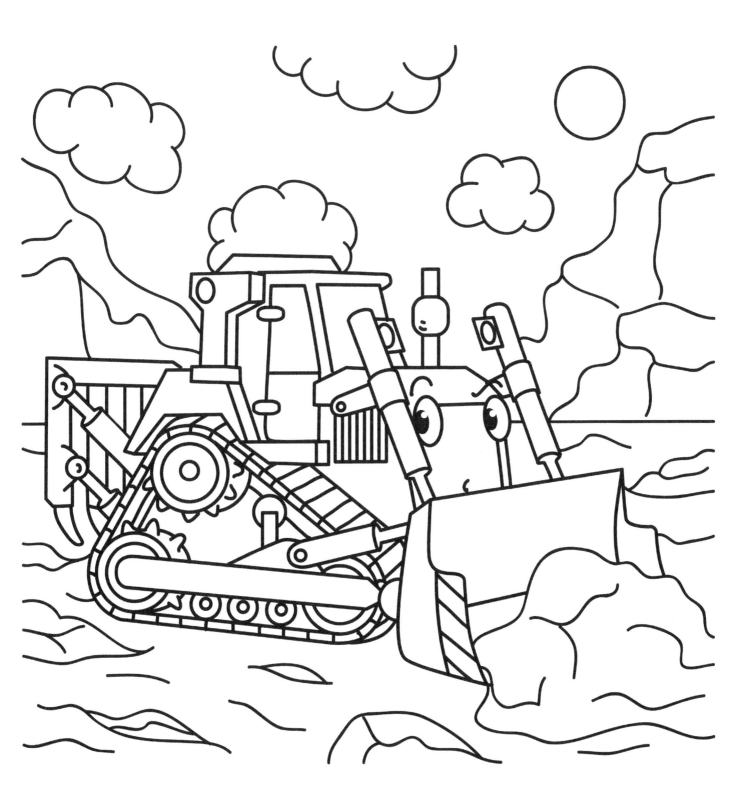

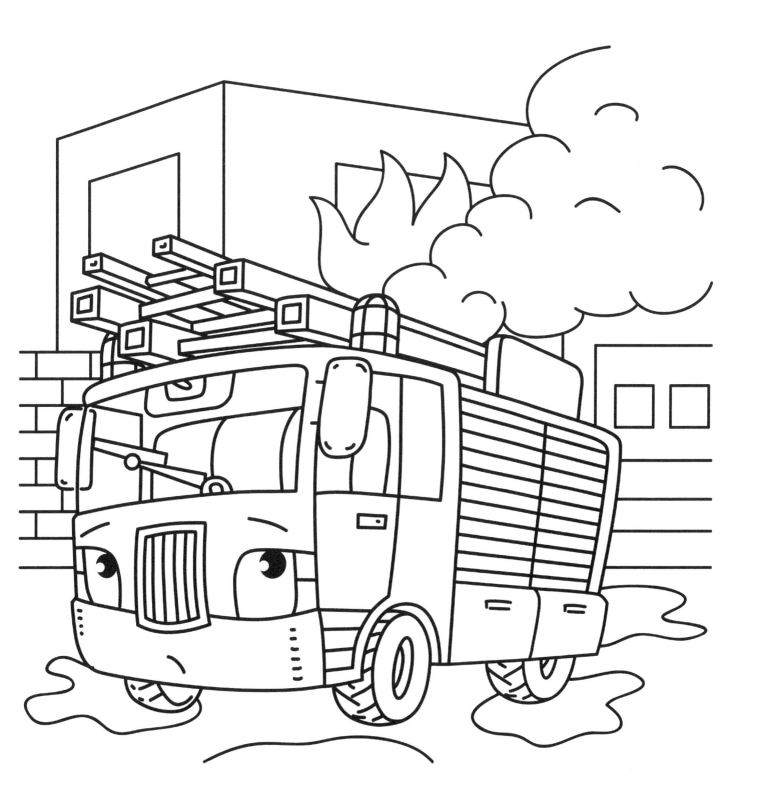

CPSIA information can be obtained
at www.ICGtesting.com
Printed in the USA
LVHW100403060521
686657LV00019BA/265